better together*

*This book is best read together, grownup and kid.

 akidsco.com

a
kids
book
about

a kids book about MONEY

by Adam Stramwasser

A Kids Co.
Editor Jelani Memory
Designer Jonathan Simcoe
Creative Director Rick DeLucco
Studio Manager Kenya Feldes
Sales Director Melanie Wilkins
Head of Books Jennifer Goldstein
CEO and Founder Jelani Memory

DK
Editor Emma Roberts
Senior Production Editor Jennifer Murray
Senior Production Controller Louise Minihane
Senior Acquisitions Editor Katy Flint
Managing Art Editor Vicky Short
Publishing Director Mark Searle

This American Edition, 2024
Published in the United States by DK Publishing
1745 Broadway, 20th Floor, New York, NY 10019

DK, a Division of Penguin Random House LLC

A catalog record for this book is available from the Library of Congress.
ISBN: 978-0-7440-9732-0

DK books are available at special discounts when purchased in bulk for
sales promotions, premiums, fund-raising, or educational use. For details, contact:
DK Publishing Special Markets, 1745 Broadway, 20th Floor, New York, NY 10019, or SpecialSales@dk.com

Printed and bound in China

www.dk.com

akidsco.com

This book was made with Forest
Stewardship Council™ certified
paper - one small step in DK's
commitment to a sustainable future.
For more information go to
www.dk.com/our-green-pledge

To Michelle and Noah.

Intro
for grownups

There's nothing like seeing kids smiling and enjoying life. But sometimes, the things we do to try to make them happy might come with some unintended consequences.

The gifts we give them, the way we respond to their wants, how we let them treat their toys, and how we talk (or don't talk) about money are all teaching them something, good or bad, about the value of things.

Money can be complicated, even for us as grownups. So, understandably, many of us avoid talking to kids about it. But the reality, whether we like it or not, is that kids are forming their own ideas about money just by watching us.

This book is designed to help you, the grownup in their life, shape those ideas and help them understand the importance of consciously saving, spending, and giving.

Hi, my name is Adam.

And this is a kids book
about money.

Let's try something...

Say:

DEE-NEH-ROH.

Congratulations, now you speak Spanish! (If you didn't already!)

"Dinero" is Spanish for...

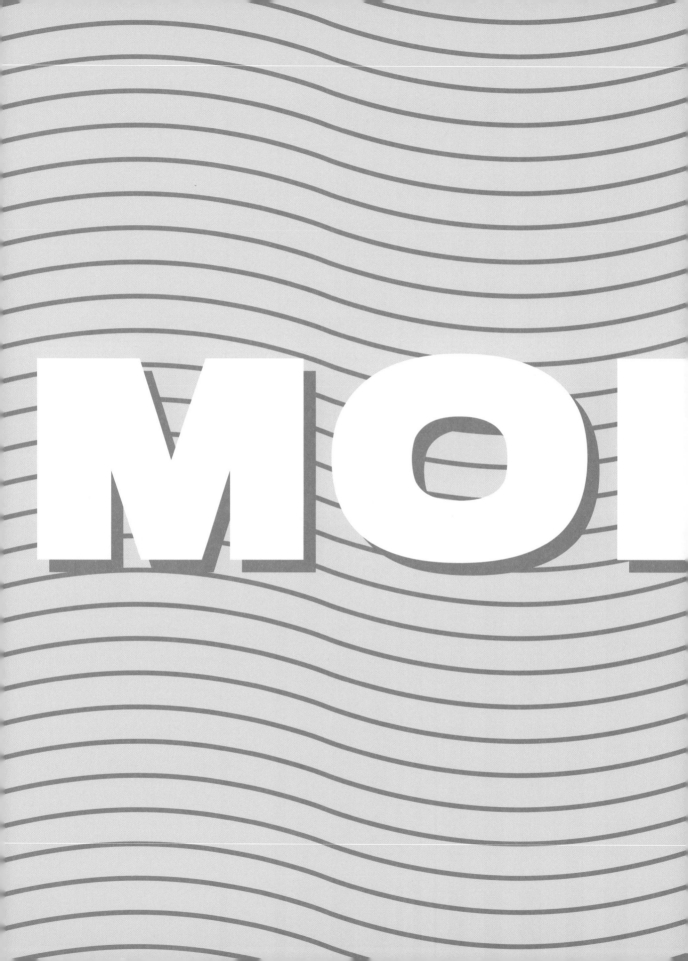

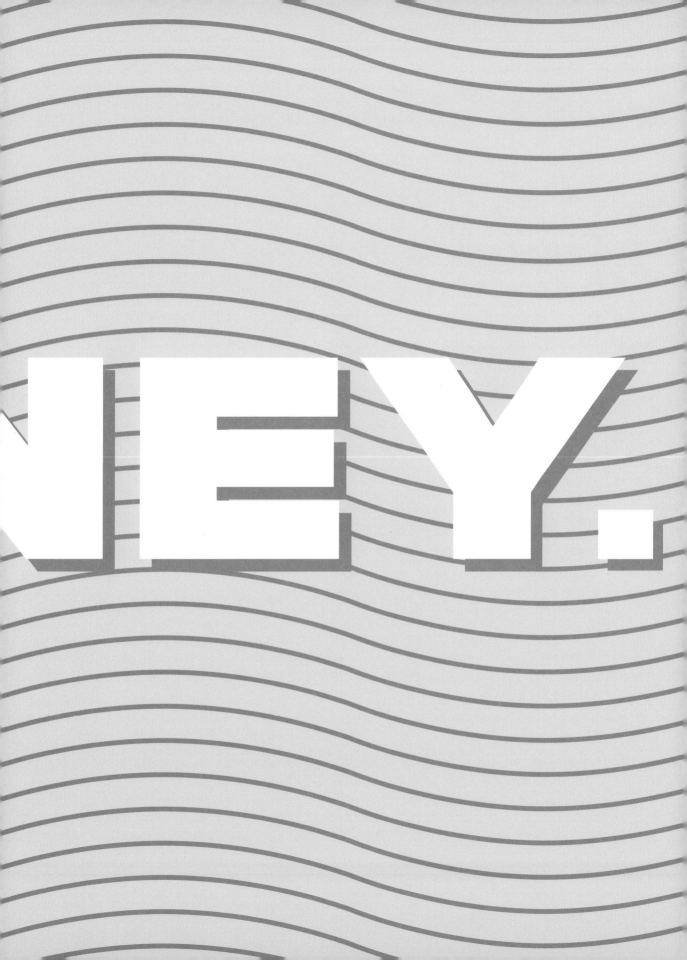

Money can be:

We can carry money:

- bills
- coins
- digital coins
- checks

- in a wallet
- on bank cards
- on a phone
- on our watch

Have you ever wondered...

where money comes from?

why we need money?

what money can buy?

how to get more money?

Money can be really

COMPLICATED,

even for grownups...

but it doesn't have to be.

Let me explain.

Money is a tool that gets us things—

things we need or want.

For example...

a grownup bought

THIS

BOOK

so you can read it!

Guess how much
MONEY they paid to buy it?

1
MILLION
DOLLARS!

(Not really, it was about 20 bucks.)

Imagine how many **BANANAS** you could buy with $20.

20, 30, 40, 100?!

FARMERS MARKET

80	Bananas
	....................$20.00

That's a lot of bananas!

Think about how many extra
chores **YOU** would
have to do...

extra

extra

extra

extra

extra

extra

extra

extra

extra

extra

to earn that **MUCH** money?
Probably a lot.*

*Note to grownup: ask your kid to do more chores ;).

You see,
money has value to
get things, both **big** and
small, that we need
or want.

So, how do you make money?

That's right, kiddo.

We can all get money
by working.

Work is when someone spends their time...

making,

doing,

selling,

teaching,

performing,

fixing,

or helping,

and in return,
they get money for it.

Work can mean being a...

babysitter,

teacher,

Uber driver,

doctor,

pilot,

baseball player,

or ballerina.

So, let's say you did extra chores around the house last month, and your grownup paid you $20.

WOO-HOO!

High-five!

You have $20 now—what should you do with it?

You could buy:

toys...$20.00

a movie ticket.................................$11.00

cheeseburgers............................$7.99

a room full of balloons..............$17.50

some socks....................................$2.99

candy...$5.00

But you can't buy everything.

Now, don't worry,
there are some
things that
do not cost
money...

like

HUGS, LAUGHS, SUNSETS, AND RAINBOWS.

But really, some things do cost a lot of money.

Like a bouncy house!

So, what can you do?

First, figure out
what you

need,

like food, clothes,
and school supplies.

Then, figure out what you

want,

like toys, candy, video games, or a castle.

Sometimes, we only have enough money for the things we need.

And we have to wait and save up for the things we want.

You're

S
M
A
R
T...

and smart kids
don't spend
all their money
all at once.

You're smart with
money when...

you **save** a little,

spend a little,

and **give** a little.

Think about it:

**if you earn $20
and you don't spend it...**

When you earn another $20, you'll have $40!

That's called **SAVING.**

Now, you could use some money to buy yourself a toy.

That's called **SPENDING.**

And buy another for a kid who doesn't have any toys.

That's called **GIVING.**

See—money isn't that complicated, right?!

So, if you can,
always try to

save,

spend,

and **give.**

As long as you do that,
having DINERO
will be FUN!

Outro
for grownups

ow that your kid is ready to invest in the stock market, you can retire and relax!

Seriously though, the conversation around money cannot stop here. Get them involved when you go grocery shopping, or have them help plan your next trip.

If you can, encourage them to be productive and earn their money, whether it's helping out more around the house or creating stuff they could sell. They'll thank you later for instilling that mindset in them.

Finally, you can help kids manage their hard-earned money by teaching them the jar system. Give them 3 clear jars. Label the 1st jar SAVING, the 2nd SPENDING, and the 3rd GIVING. Have them put money in each jar, with a specific goal in mind. This goal-based system is one of the most effective ways to manage money. Not just for kids, but for adults as well. And you thought this was just a "kids" book about money, huh?

About The Author

Adam Stramwasser (he/him) was born and raised in Venezuela. At 20, he left his home, family, and friends in pursuit of a better future. Growing up in a country bogged down by political and economic instability, it was difficult to work towards goals other than providing food and shelter.

As an immigrant in the United States, Adam learned an important lesson about the value of work and being smart with money. Adam says, "Living in the present is much more enjoyable when you know you're also building a future."

After working as an investment advisor for wealthy people in New York City, Adam now leads a movement to help the Hispanic community design and build their financial future so they can fully live their present.

 @stramhacks   @stramhacks

Made to empower.

a kids book about racism
by Jelani Memory

a kids book about ANXIETY
by Ross Szabo

a kids book about DISABILITY
by Kristine Napper

a kids book about IMAGINATION
by LEVAR BURTON

a kids book about belonging
by Kevin Carroll

a kids book about failure
by Dr. Laymon Hicks

a kids book about GRATITUDE
by Ben Kenyon

a kids book about LIFE ONLINE
by Dave S. Anderson & Blake Fleischacker

a kids book about body image
by Rebecca Alexander

a kids book about IMMIGRATION
by MJ Calderon

a kids book about EMPATHY
by Daron K. Roberts

a kids book about GENDER
by Dale Mueller

Discover more at akidsco.com